The Old Rob Poems

For Lee & Rob,
for reading through a the
mountain. Wonderful cabin!

Love,

Joe

25 April 2015
(Morkfest weekend)

The Old Rob Poems

John Lane

New Native Press
2014

Acknowledgements:
"Old Rob Stays Home" as "The Idiot Magnet" in *Tar River Poetry*
"Old Rob Goes Blind" in *Alkali Flats*
"Old Rob Looks for Eric Rudolph" as "Up Worry Hut," and "Old Rob Plants His
  Last Allotment," in *South Carolina Poetry Anthology*
"Old Rob Charts the Progress of Bees" in *Poetry Hotel*
"Old Rob Goes to Wal-Mart" in *Rivendell*
"Old Rob and the Free-Range Chickens" in *Story South*
"Old Rob and the Luna Moths" as "Lunas" in *The Cortland Review*
"Old Rob and the Spider's Doorway" in *Katuah*.
"Old Rob Remembers the Shine" in *The James Dickey Review*
"Old Rob's Neighbor Clears a View" in *Quarter After Eight.*

Cover and text photos by Thomas Crowe & John Lane

Copy Editor: Nan Watkins
Book Designer: Thomas Crowe

Printed at: TPS, Newton, IL

New Native Press books and broadsides are published
for Thomas Crowe by New Native Press. Orders
or inquiries may be addressed to: NNP, PO Box 2554,
Cullowhee, NC 28723. Email:newnativepress@hotmail.com.
website: www.newnativepress.org

Library of Congress Catalog Card Number: 2014947811

ISBN: 1-883197-40-6

10 9 8 7 6 5 4 3 2 1

CONTENTS

A Note on *The Old Rob Poems*:

    I began writing *The Old Rob Poems* about fifteen years ago when I was spending long stretches of every summer on John's Creek in Jackson County, North Carolina. I'd bought a piece of land from a friend and settled into the life of an occasional weekend and summer visitor from the flat lands. I'd been reading Jim Wayne Miller's *Briar* poems, and Kathryn Stripling Byer's "Alma" poems from her book *Black Shawl*. Though I love these poems I kept wondering, "What's the contemporary male equivalent of Briar or Alma in Jackson County, NC?"

    What I settled on was Old Rob, a character based loosely on a real mountain neighbor I knew when I first bought my place on John's Creek. The real Rob was a retired logger who dabbled in real estate. What struck me as we talked on his porch was how he was sort of a seam character, someone passing from the old mountain world into a purely modern one. That created a fun persona and situation to play with. At the same time that I started on these poems I began to build a cabin on my place on the site of the original structure from the 19th century. I engaged a young mountain man to help me build it, someone who knew the old ways of framing what he called "a saw mill shack." Listening to this man gave me some of the stories that became Rob's experiences. In the end Rob emerged with a life and a voice of his own and became charged with my own experiences in the mountains.

-John Lane
Spartanburg, SC, 2014

for David Lee

"They die hard, the old ways, in the mountains."

—Horace Kephart

Q: Can you tell me about the hermit who lived up in the cove?
A: John, he weren't no hermit he were just an old man.

OLD ROB STAYS HOME

Old Rob didn't like to go to town, even Sylva.
He was born into Kephart's "branch water people"
who stayed close-by the wild geranium,
and let the sound of falling poplar leaves
guide them through their common purposes.

Their industry was what each day provided,
a log down on a high ridge, a dynamite charge,
making a little shine. Rob still believed
in sitting close to the road and noting how
the day releases each hour as it will,
not according to some clock tuned by hand.

When Rob was young he asked his brother why
all those people wanted to walk Main Street
and eat food not cooked by their mamas.
"There's a big old idiot magnet buried under
every First National Bank in America,"
his brother explained. The wisdom suited
Old Rob so he's always stayed away.

OLD ROB LOOKS FOR ERIC RUDOLPH

The ATF agents came looking for Rudolph
up John's Creek. They found rhododendron thickets.
They shouldered M-16s and wore camouflage
against the green hell of the high mountains.
John's Creek let them in, and then swallowed them
like it has everything else—the Mississippians,
the Cherokee, Old Rob's great grandfather
who rode a mule up the hollow the first time.

College students in trailers near the hollow's mouth
didn't stop the agents. They came on up the road
past the last Floridians who build on the view lot ridges,
on up to where Old Rob and his people have lived
since the settlement. There's two water crossings
to get to Old Rob's land, and a bend in the road
so deep it will put a crease in any car longer than
a wagon. Old Rob still likes it that way.

Rob says he's seen an Indian princess
up in a laurel sprawl high near the parkway.
He's heard her brown baby cry too. On John's Creek
such sounds blend with the slow rain, the luna moth's
wings at night, the salamander leaving a watery
trail through the falling branch. "He could be
under any stone," Old Rob says of Rudolph.
"He could be hole up in some hidden Indian cave."
Up John's Creek, anything's possible. The road goes
nowhere but higher. The forest grows greener
and deeper with each twisted mile of two-track.

Some say there's little people up John's Creek,
from before the Indians. Building one house
a man with a backhoe opened up tiny little
tunnels all over the hill side, perfectly round
and only four feet high. He told no one but me,
not out of fear as much as respect for the mystery.

See that curling tail of rock dust? That's
the government men leaving John's Creek.
Rob knows they'll be back, but not today or tomorrow.

They looked for Indians like Tsali up here,
taxes, Confederate conscripts, and corn whiskey.
Found nothing but the lonesome call of the hoot owl,
the circle of the dogwood blossom, the drooping
trillium in bloom all over John's Creek in the spring.

OLD ROB STUDIES THE PHLOX

> *"To make children grow fat,*
> *bathe them in a root infusion."*
> —old Cherokee medicine

Outside, the stream in the laurel hell
inclines toward the lower John's Creek valley.
Summer phlox softens farm hillsides it covers.

Each year Rob softens too. His belly gone slack,
mind drawn like the phlox more toward mush,
legs bowed like the bear on the ridge,
chest sagging lower than two tender hills.

Garden phlox, fall aster, laxative, boil balm,
this bloom will be old Rob's coffin wreath,
lying in visitation in the house no longer standing.

He bathes each morning in this hillside infusion.
He met the lavender eyes of phlox
staring past the valley of middle age.
He grew old and fat gazing at nodding phlox stalks
in adolescent June, almost solstice.

OLD ROB CUTTING BRUSH

"And trees came closer with a denser shade."
— Theodore Roethke

Mid-day, cutting rhododendron in the creek,
turning a low branch, Rob careens into the white
fairy space of the resting, day-slowed luna moth.
Four inches of pale green translucent wings,
the luna moth motors the black air with twin sensors.

*

A hidden grouse ravaging the maple silence,
a hip-shot from deep brush as the dog works
side-long the hill-side. The mealy humid air
tunneled by bird-flight. The calculated advance
through the trees. The dog's shattered surprise.

*

The small shapes dipping; dimpled poplar shade.
A creek bank veering into spongy loam.
Two young walnut saplings collapsed by blight.
Residual slope and the even plane of a logging road.
The locust tilting toward a boulder scrawled with moss.

*

Saplings are dying piecemeal, scrapping in a forest
of white pine, hemlock, groves of fragrant cedar.
Rob keeps the company of the soft-fleshed, attends
the resiny theater of slow growth, old decay.
Each day is a door, the piles of brush heating up in the sun.

OLD ROB AND THE BRUSH PILE

Placed dead in the light all things
dry out, break down, open up to the air.
Poplar saplings, straight as paddle shafts,
snap when pulled the wrong way.

Birch bark grown fragile and sun-baked
sloughs off in his gloved hands.
The dogwood stunted
among poplars, the scrawny limbs hacked.
It never bloomed in the deep shade
so Rob cut it down.

Wild grape vines grow brittle,
cut through to lounge a winter away
in direct, immediate mid-day sun.
They fight like cornered black snakes,
find life in Rob's clumsy struggle.

OLD ROB'S PHILOSOPHY

"Every force evolves a form."
— old Shaker saying

Rob's field is hell-bent on being forest.
He's hell-bent on forest being field.
The answer's somewhere in the middle,
between the space field's forces fill
and what his human form can yield.

OLD ROB'S NEIGHBOR CLEARS A VIEW

One of Rob's new Florida neighbors cuts down all
the white oaks blocking his fine distances. At three
thousand feet, so go the locusts and the birch as well.
The tulip poplars, down with them, after all, deciduous
means "Let it drop." Drop the buckeye, the basswood,
the silver bell. Drop the big hemlock grown on this ridge
a hundred years, left by loggers as a boundary tree.
Let drop the buggy white pine.

Lop the limbs with chainsaw, oily rag, bar wrench, leather gloves.
Oil the bar. Cut the trunks into cord wood, quartered and stacked
in the pickup bed. Trim back the rhododendron, mountain laurel,
redbud, serviceberry, flowering dogwood, hydrangea, dog hobble.

Plow the slope. Burn the dead limbs. Plant grass and root out
the fringed phacelia, the strawberry bush, profusion of ferns,
creeping and crawling vines, cat briar and poison ivy, mosses,
fungi, algae. Plant azaleas. Empty bags of potting soil mixed
with vermiculite. Add cow manure. Top with cypress mulch.
Sink a well, a creosoted light pole with street light, septic line
(pull out the remaining roots), travel trailer, graveled drive,
covered deck, screened and lighted.

Rob's new neighbor calls this mountain living. Calls this vacation
home, get-away, investment property, tax shelter, inheritance.
Beats all summer long at mountain forest, edging out his yard.
Walks his property line, looking for corner stakes tipped in red.
Waters his lawn. Rounds up poison ivy, blackberry bramble.
Edges flower beds. Weedeats Queen Anne's lace along drive.
Admires the distances green, sometimes hazy, sometimes clear.

OLD ROB GOES TO WAL-MART

In the parking lot Rob tells his niece
he's never seen so much flat land
without a crop of corn growing.
So it is Old Rob enters the country
of Wal-Mart as a curious mountain man.
It's after midnight. Rob's niece works
the third shift nursing at the hospital
and this is when she could bring her uncle
down from John's Creek to see the store.

They enter the electric doors and a man
old as Rob hands them a cart. "Take it,"
he says, like it's a sacrament to the tongue
when Old Rob hesitates before him.
The niece pushes the cart past the stacks
and explains to Old Rob the plastic coolers,
lawn chairs, tiki lanterns to dope
the summer's rare hollow mosquito.
"It's time for the Florida people to buy,
buy, buy their essentials for life in these hills,"
she says, and it's true. The aisles are wide
as a logging road for two shoppers to pass.

But Old Rob's not here to buy. He just wants
to see the Wal-Mart before his eyes go milky,
see what the great-grandchildren are talking
about on Sundays. He notices niece walks aisles
the way his great-grandfather must have
walked under chestnuts rising 300 feet above,
the ground thick with the year's mast.
Even she buys a few things, potato chips,
paper towels in an eight pack, a new mop.

"It's always full of Indians this hour,"
she whispers to Rob as a Cherokee family
walks past with a full cart. "It's all that
gambling money." And Old Rob sees she's
right. In every aisle there are dark-skinned
people in brightly colored new clothes
like the hollow fall has settled on the store
three months early— red, yellow, ocher.
"I've seen it all," he says. "Now I'm ready

to go back home." They go through check-out
and his niece pays with a credit card.
Old Rob fingers the few pieces of silver
in his pocket and wonders if any Cherokee
keep to the old ways, how a dollar buys
what a dollar gets, how a man stays sane.

OLD ROB REMEMBERS WORKING IN THE MILL

How piedmont pines always had a blood-red moon above.
How there was always a barking dog.
How for honest work he walked the spinning room.

How gravel sounded under a tire, needles on a windshield.
How cicadas sawed pulpwood out of pine.
How somebody cut that dog loose.

How behind his house was a dead-end road.
How down there, miles of woods too.
How on the highway a truck shifted into third.

How it was working a third shift long as hell.
How every movement was a machine, out, down, and inside.
How he ate too many pinto beans and cans of salmon.

OLD ROB AND THE FREE-RANGE CHICKENS

In Rob's childhood the roosters in the hollow
had fat yellow combs. They strutted in the yards,
free of wire fences. Two roosters belonged to Uncle Tommy,
two more to his other uncles, Bobby and Billy.
Most days the hens circulated from yard to yard,
tended nests under the porch, built from scattered hay
gathered from the old useless fields and plucked
from the spiked racks of the stalled threshing machines.

Each brown egg, a breakfast orb flecked with shit and straw.
On Sunday mornings Uncle Tommy appeared with an ax,
hanging loosely at his side. The gregarious hens hid
when they heard his door slam, two cabins down.

One hen each week startled by conjunction of ax and block.
Bloody heads rotted in the wire grass, the eyes gone by noon.
In Rob's dreams poultry still careens, small brown storms,
through his front yard swept clean by his young mama.

OLD ROB PLANTS HIS LAST ALLOTMENT

1.
When winter grabbed hold of John's Creek
Old Rob piled the year's brush
in long rows, lit the dry locust branches,
withered maple saplings, the tops of stove
wood oaks. The dead wood caught.
As the last pile flamed out, Rob watched
grey ash swirling in the wind like snow.

2.
Burly Knob humped beyond Rob's field,
seemed ready to bend under February cold.
Dry weeds from last year's season covered
rock piles in the quarter acre field
Rob's son still let him plant in the old ways.

3.
Ash killed the seeds of weeds sleeping below.
In March Rob started seeds, tearing open each
government pack, Kentucky 101 and Tennessee.
In the barn he filled little Dixie Cups with dark
hollow earth, pushed each seed thumb deep.

4.
Rob's mule was old as he was, moved
slow in the rising heat after the last frost.
When May showed they moved one last time
together between the rock piles, broke the land,
prepared the bottom field for the last planting.

OLD ROB GOES FISHING

for James Kilgo

It was into the trickle tributaries
that Old Rob liked to chase speckle trout.
His Saturday mornings meant fishing.
He'd grab a supple cane pole slashed
from the bottom field and tie on some
line, pocket some hooks, and off he'd go.

He knew early that a can of sweet corn
in his overall pocket was bait enough.
What he wanted was fish in the pan
or canned standing shoulder-to-shoulder
in a mason jar for a deep winter meal.

Up the north boulder trail Old Rob
climbed into the highest laurel hells.
Down on his knees he'd crawl to reach
the seeps where rivulets welled up
on the flattened shoulders of Burly Knob.

He'd start fishing in the cold shadows,
descending all day through one branch's
swift meander to another, chasing water
downhill to where it met some more
and took on more, grew swift and bold.

By the time Rob reached John's Creek's
definite crease, he'd filled a wet
poke with little dark and cream
speckle trout. On the porch he opened
his sack, admired the fish working
fat-lipped mouths like a chorus.

Old Rob laughed the first time
a flat-land angler in his Forerunner
bumped up John's Creek looking for
native brookies in the back country.
The flatlander's "back-of-beyond"
was Rob's front yard, swept clean
to the line of hemlocks and laurel.

With creel and rod the young man
set out over hill and through hollow
and Rob watched him disappear
from the cabin's front porch.

About dark the man returned
and Rob asked how he did
with the little speckle fish
up on the Government Land among
the cliffs, clouds, and springs.
"I'm angling for native brook trout,"
the man explained. "Catch and release,"
his creel empty, leaving without one fish.

Rob sat and pondered the sense
of walking all that way without
speckle trout gasping in a sack,
crying out for grease and pan.
It was Rob's first hint of change
to come. When he grew too old
to climb up on Burly Knob
and chase the run-off down
his niece brought in a foam cooler
full of frozen nursery rainbows
and canned them for the old man.

They never tasted right to him,
the flavor lacked some wildness
Rob could touch with his tongue.
His niece laughed when granddaddy
complained and said, "trout's trout."

OLD ROB CHARTS THE PROGRESS OF BEES

Bees worked the fall wild flowers
on the top of Burly Knob.
The labor of their wings
was lost to the greasy vowels of back hoes,
graders, two chain saws below.

First time, five decades before,
Rob stood here looking out so far
through clear air he swear all that sprawled
below were small farms, the back door screens
of mountain farmers, and the gears
grinding on someone's old pick up.

Time taught Rob how change
can come: gradual, like erosion,
at an inch a year, or in the rumble
of catastrophe— like a natural dam
breaking, the water pushing
ancient landscapes clean.

He's had it with the pretty places
sold to the highest bid,
rhododendron cleared for condos.
Soon they'll cut off that trail
he walked in to see so far,
put up a club house there.

If this is progress he wants none;
give him the progress of bees
beside this endless drop and view,
nectar from fall flowers
the hundred-thousandth time
since things changed that much.

Who owns a mountain, a glade,
or a view sprawling on forever?
Rob's sick of what's now called
progress and low-land greed.

OLD ROB TENDS HIS GARDEN

Weeds sprout inside the wire fence
around Rob's garden. Their green pods
nod indolently in any breeze.
Sun flowers gesture toward a yellow sun.

The high, 100. The low, 80.
Peppers are all that bloom untroubled.
In April, Old Rob had so much hope,
beat daily at the creeping weeds with a hoe.

August tomatoes are small, hard,
and garlic rots in stony ground.
How to water, when water pools,
then dries, softening nothing?

OLD ROB KILLS A COPPERHEAD

With the snake's tail
 buzzing against dry leaves,
Rob sets about clearing
a copperhead
from the yard.

With hoe in hand
he creeps up
as the grandkids
watch from the
the porch.

Up close, Rob
admires the snake's
pure, cold attention:

matching poison
eyes, unblinking,
eternal in its
stare, a tongue
like fire rolling
out from this
angel come back
to draw all close
to what they fear.

Then the hoe
comes down,
cleaves head
from the hourglass.
Rob takes up
the serpent's body
with the crook
and feeds it
to the hogs.

OLD ROB GATHERS PERSIMMONS

Given one good frost
bitter fruit turns
pink, drops from leafless
limbs. Plump pods, simple
fruit, persimmons, common
as apples in Rob's backyard
economy. He stirs through
raccoon scat in October,
sees seeds smooth as river stones.

Rob goes to gathering
with the coons. Strains
and cooks a tangy jam.
Store-bought?
Give Rob the ripe
persimmons, smelling
of the season
that burnt them changed.

OLD ROB AND THE LUNA MOTHS

Scattered wings the color of new leaves—
a starling flies in and plucks a live one
off the barn door's lintel. Old Rob spots three
more clinging to the building's rough boards.

One street light's brought them in over night.
One week of love and then they're gone—
a ribbon-thin clutch of eggs left behind.

OLD ROB REMEMBERS FARMING THE BOTTOMS

No one grows corn in the bottoms.
Caney Fork meanders past in its steep banks
past saplings, over fallen saw timber

undercut sharply by falling pewter current.
Rob walks the trail, follows his hounds
who follow his grandsons on their bikes.

It's muddy, and the bottoms
soaked through from recent winter rains.
Mud catches in the hexes on Rob's boots.

He carries the bottoms home,
thinks the high ridges coming down
scraping his dirty soles at the door.

OLD ROB LISTENS TO CICADAS

They scrape the underside off the day,
the hulks of their long sleep sloughed
into the leaves of green summer oaks.

They repent for his somnolence, as inside
the cabin Rob sleeps while they prickle
the shadows with their simple notes.

They harry the dawn, then stop soon after.
And during the day their small springs wind
back to silence as humidity fills the air.

They cling to the backs of black limbs,
and when the wind passes in the hollow
they sit silent and wait for the dusk.

OLD ROB REMEMBERS LOGGING BURLY KNOB

It were in '49 or '50 I cranked that first power saw and the rattlesnakes come out of the hills. They thought it were another snake singing and they come from everywhere. That year I cut the whole mountainside up to the Brown place, right down to Uncle Bob's cabin.

They was standing dead dry chestnuts three and four feet thick covered the whole mountain up to the ridge beyond. I cut all them standing dead trees and the black rattlers come out of hibernation that winter and crawled the hollows with all that singing they heard. I looked down and one was crawling through my legs and over there they'd be another. You know they ain't no rattlesnakes up in there at your place now. You got plenty of copperheads and you got to watch them too 'cause they'll kill you just as quick if they hit a vein. They's plenty of copperheads and 'sang too.

They's a little ivy patch up there where you go down into yorn place and they's 'sang apleany in that patch. I seen it beforn I was blind. I couldn't see nothing up there now. I one time got 22 roots under one butternut tree up there up at yorn place and I wasn't too good at spotting it like some of these fellers.

It's a hundred dollar a pound and they sell it overseas, so hit must be something. They was probably up there looking it when they stole your Weedeater and looking at you too. I got a root in there that Queen boy brought me and I cut off a little piece and chew it and it does work some on me. Oh yeah, I logged all these mountains and we didn't clear it like they do now. Took all the trees over 16 inches and this land will grow a crop of saw timber ever 30 years if you don't take the little ones. Ever 30 years. They's saw timber up there on your place already and I took the trees off. You know when a man's getting $100 a 1000 that's a lot of money on 240 acres. I took a lot of trees off that mountain and there's still plenty up there. You know you got good water and four or five good lots on that piece I sold Tom Crowe.

It were broom sedge from your place all the way down to the road. My daddy used to have a corner up on that road above you and I came up there once when I was still a boy with my daddy and Uncle Bob Brown was down at his cabin cutting wood for his fire and my daddy yelled down to him and said, 'Uncle Bob, do you know where my corner is?' and Uncle Bob yelled back, 'I know exactly whur that corner is 'cause my daddy set it' and he was right and Uncle Bob came up and showed us and they was 13 acres— I seed the old deed written out years ago— that the Browns had deeded to those two boys— Uncle Bob and his brother— below us 'cause it was such good land and that's the land you got now.

OLD ROB AND THE COLD COMING ON

Rob's warmth grows small as a kerosene flame
among walls of blazing fall sassafras,
purple asters, tulip poplar weathered
yellow by the chilly air. He takes the hound

for an early walk, climbs the old logging
road up Burly Knob, slips through runnels
left by the slow October rain,
the lapped debris of mountain wind.

He climbs to the vacant Florida People's place,
spots a light floating in the dawn-distance,
like the Brown Mountain lights of legend
far away, misty, greasy, remote.

Old Rob thinks it's his mountain spirit
come for him returned through the rain,
small persistent light at dawn.

OLD ROB FINDS SOME CLOTHES

Rob pulled his great-granddaughter over
at the big bend in the Tuckaseigee River
where the county sets up for trash.
The three big green collectors were full
to overflowing, like bins of wheat stored

for threshing—and just on top in paper grocery sacks
somebody had dropped a man's clothes
piled high and Rob couldn't pass them by—
"Either he's dead or lost so much weight they
can't even cinch up," Rob said as he stepped out,
shuffled over to sort the lucky windfall.

His niece was appalled—
how could he look through somebody else's trash?
"Not trash, honey," Rob reasoned, gesturing far and wide
to nearby hills, rills, and hollows. "Just God's bounty
passed on for all to share."

Rob heaved his old knotty forearm deep
in the first sack and rooted past white dress shirts
and snagged what he knew by the buckles
to be a set of overalls and fished them out—
"Looka here," he smiled. "Not my size exactly, but close
enough," holding high water short up on Old Rob's shins.

OLD ROB AND THE SCRAP MAN

Pushing his cart up Worryhut's winding two-track
the scrap man announced his arrival with a whoop,
beating an old tin pan with a broken wooden spoon.
Rob anticipated his weekly rounds, heaped hoops
of barrels, the staves gone to rot, rusted barbed
wire curls, a stew pot scraped thin a hundred years
by soup ladles, iron skillets cracked in a cabin fire,
anything worth a nickel to the old-time scrap man.

The scrap man's gone the way of seed salesmen,
town criers, the milk man, sawyers, ash hoppers,
soap makers, herb gatherers, cellar holes, shuck moppers,
homemade dyers, cobblers, corn grinders, blacksmiths,
itinerate preachers setting up revival tents in a lower field.
These days new scrap men sell air conditioner copper,
add tonnage signs stole off Worry Hut's one-lane bridges.
Rob's niece has put her air handler in a chain link cage,
and her uncle eats off plastic, cooks mostly in a microwave.

OLD ROB WALKS INTO THE GORGE

Rob went deep in the gorge
where he knew waterfalls conspire with air.
Spiders had knitted doors all along the trail.
He broke through every one.

Soon Old Rob dropped a thousand feet,
the road up there somewhere,
flanked by dry ridges.

Below, along the Tuckaseigee he found
rails from an old logging line rusted
among ferns and gray granite
ledges pocked with drill bits bent
level with the stone.

But among such a residue
of history, Rob chose gold-flecked salamanders.
He could see them moving in the wet cracks
of the shaded gorge wall itself.

It was these creatures he had come for.
They drew his attention like a thread from the gut
of a spider. He wrapped the moment with his attention.
He spun his heritage out of such moments.

OLD ROB AND THE SUN

Old Rob watches his brindle hound
track the sun through a griddle of shade
and dappled light. The porch is warm
where sun wedges the ground, trailing
moments through the day.
It's winter warmth she's after, and Rob
remembers when his limbs held
heat too. But now he and the old dog
have similar habits—Rob turning his rocker
on the porch most south-facing afternoons,
and the dog meandering from swept stoop
to bleached boards to find the sun.
When the heat's gone and the short day
retreats, Robs goes inside and hoards warmth
from a space heater's flame, family
quilts, and darned long red underwear.
The hound curls tight as a pine knot
and holds back the cold until dawn.

OLD ROB AND THE GYRATIONS OF THE AGES

Disciplined stars still swirl in the evening sky
and Rob remembers their paths like fissures
opening on the dark skull of heaven.
He remembers the full moon like a cotton bole,
and the meteors returning, flung on a flexible
arc across middens of light, the Milky Way.

Down at Judaculla Rock tourists spread
picnic blankets on the stone, drink wine,
eat fried chicken where the Old Ones scratched
an alphabet of signs on a weathered soapstone slab.
Rob planted by the stars like the Old Ones, grew corn,
then tobacco as floods rose and fell, furrowed
year-by-year, shucked, tucked his bins
for winter, feeding penned stock and cabined kin.

Now transplanted irrigated tomatoes
grow like giant strawberries in ordered rows
picked by squads of Mexicans driving
U-Hauls up and back from Florida truck farms.
In their mixed blood runs Aztec and Toltec lineage
who traded corn north to the Mississippians,
then the Cherokee, and on to Rob's Scot forebears.

The dark fields take it all, stitched back and forward
with the hands of workers and seeds of simple
plants for sauces and the people's sustenance.
Some plots already sprout houses and yards,
but Rob's too blind to care, too far up the hollow
for flat land, too old to see good dark dirt
gone to fescue and store-bought azaleas.

OLD ROB REMEMBERS HIS BROTHER'S DEATH

Rob's stories were like
track, moving memory's freight
between now and then:
As a child they placed crossed
safety pins, not pennies,
on the train tracks and then
the old steam train
had crushed them flat
like little scissors that
couldn't cut. And then

as if memory were
a switch box, Rob's brother
was catching a ride
on a moving 1915 freight,
behind their uncle's house
in Sylva, and the boy

missed the ladder,
and then as always,
ended up under the wheels
in Rob's mind, legs
cut through again.

OLD ROB GOES BLIND

For Old Rob there is no pause between silences
when the crickets stop, so he anticipates neighbors,
friends, strangers, meter readers, dogs and storms
as diversions in the blowing hall of darkening space.

Growing blind as the autumn grass grows dull green,
growing still and stern as the boulders tumbled by frost
in the hollow, Old Rob persists with morning and evening
chores of tending what passes on the paved road.

Sight is no mountain poplar whose tulip blossoms return,
soft orange and green. It is more like the hillside alum cave
abandoned to cat briar and poison ivy late last century.

He measures the lengthening shadows, trees and light
pushed into crevasses of dark mass and ringing shade.
He sits in a lawn chair, the tar yellow on his fingers
from years of smoking, and probes with memory
and patience the cricket-loud edges where the road
once passed his view and continues out of the cove.

OLD ROB REMEMBERS THE SHINE

Rob always tucked his still in a laurel hell
hard on the sharp flank of Doubletop Mountain
where John's Creek took its leave of clouds.
No more adept conjurer ever turned clear
branch water and cord wood into silver shine.
His daddy's simple recipe passed down
from Scotch forebears, replacing ancient
barley mash with corn from his own field.

They called it lightning, but shine cleared
the darkness way longer than a wrinkle
of light on a horizon collapsing to the west.
If medicine was what made you better off,
then Rob was doctor to the whole cove,
his prescription jug ladled and cooled
among sheltered roots of an old sassafras.

Then all through the hills the flammable
bathtub stew of Sudafed, phosphorus,
and acid took the place of old-time shine.
One fall they even found a meth lab hidden
under the counter of the Moonshiner's Mini-Mart.
By the time crystal inched up the hollow
Rob's still was rusted away in the creek,
his recipe for moonshine long forgotten
among the rusted rings of tin barrels
and shadow thoughts cooking in his head.

OLD ROB'S CONFESSION

Forgive me Lord, for I have seen the ruby-throated
hummingbird fly from cardinal flower to coreopsis.
And I have heard the hoot owl's single note
in these particular woods. I confess the sun is late
today and there's no sign that it will
relieve your high expectations of morning.

Forgive me if I am not ashamed that store-bought
clocks are less trustworthy than the dawn.
Every morning I wake to aqua-tailed lizards
along the porch rail. I praise the short lives
of the cold-blooded and naturally blue.
In your wisdom you have sown abundant blessings
among the caterpillars, broad-headed skinks,
the cardinal's feathers vanished from his red head.

OLD ROB LISTENS TO THE CREEK RISE

Old Rob didn't have to watch The Weather Channel
to know the creek was eating its banks.
He sat blind in his split-birch porch rocker
and listened to the voice of flood coming down the valley.

The air was full of frenzy—Rob could smell the mud-
muddled rush of current across John's Creek Road.
He felt the porch shimmy a little with the rising surge
as rainfall gathered, ran in sheets, plunged through culverts,
crawled the crooked channel in a turmoil.

With the storm stalled over Rich Mountain, Rob imagined clouds
billowing and tumbling from the summit as they had seventy
summers before. Rob could not see it, but he still knew the dark
hover of a storm over the peak, the spars of balsam snagging
clouds on the steep wooded slopes.

Water finds its way in John's Creek, as it always had.
The creases deepen—the willows, streamside
lose their hold and collapse in field mud suspended
in a downpour of mountain rain.

What trout survive eddy safely behind the biggest boulders. Cows
and mules walk up to the ridgetop, escape the creek's
caterwauling. The blue heron sits perplexed and hungry as the
creek's surface turns too red to see through.

Next day, when the creek sleeps once more in its bed,
Old Rob walks with his cane to the stream side—
he stands there, listens to the sound drying cane makes
lifting back in place after all that wild water passes over.

OLD ROB IN DEEP WINTER

Like a train from the north
the cool snap stops at the station.
Fall is a bucket dropped deep
in the year's old well and this day
is the shallow tin dipper.

What warm-blooded beast
has now turned home?
What worm has slid back
to its deep hole?

Rob looks to the sky for signs.
He digs among the rubble
of summer for something whole.

OLD ROB AND THE SPIDER'S DOORWAY

In the old stone well house
a garden spider spun a door
where one fell from the hinges.

The roof, gone, the wide plank boards
wasted in the grass, the place
left open to light and rain.

Rob wanted to walk through, to break
the light strands, a night's spinning,
but stands instead just past
 the fieldstone wall.

Rob has always wanted to enter empty
rooms, now this one,
closed off by a web and air above.

If Rob crossed this threshold
he would rise
above the broken ceiling beams
to wait in the white, furrowed sky.

OLD ROB SIMPLY LISTENS

Rob asked his niece if fog
descending from Burly Nob
was a cloud that had lost its way
from heaven to ground, and she said,
"That white ghost is the inside
of a rabbit's nest, a cotton bole
abandoned, a grave dressing of sand."

Rob quizzed her again, this time
on hickory cracked by storms,
the wooly backs of caterpillars
and what they had to say about winter:
"A crone dead on a hillside, and an army of wooly
wanderers headed up high."

In his blindness Rob sat on the porch
and their conversations truthed the hollow,
filled his head with the girl's playful observations.

"What about the pignut just fell?"
"God's own sign," she said.
"It's the way heaven has of waking."

OLD ROB AND THE LOCUST

Old Rob lived his life with the persistence
of locust. He was like an old post set deep
in a dark hole, the bark long gone.
The durability of his mountain days
was no different than the rafters in his
'bacca barn, the stakes he shaped to
hold his springy stock fence.

Before Rob died he counted
his grandchildren, like little locust
sprouts in his backfield, the fallow one
where the cattle can't graze.
They grow up every summer
paying no heed to the absence of shade.
Sprouts, runners from Rob's line,
pushing out green leaves and black thorns.

The honey of Rob's days was dark
like the honey the little black bees
spin in April from the long white blooms.
When Old Rob died his casket was made
from a big locust the wind brought down
at the end of John's Creek. He told his niece,
"Cut broad boards at the sawmill,
join 'em good. I'll be happy when the time
comes, sunk deep in that dark locust box."

OLD ROB'S HANDS

Rice paper and chopsticks.
The last branches bleached in the sun.
The broken legs of small sparrows.
Slots through which we see another world.
Bent twigs from last night's mountain storm.
Real pain and long suffering.
Soon placed across his chest.

THE BEAR

Remembering Old Rob

Crossed the road
three miles down Caney Fork,
a young one, maybe
male, head down,
loping from thicket
brush to willow swamp,
bent on some rush
of bear intuition.

And Rob, old bear
at 75, still big, hairy
head come forward
that last time
to open the screen door,
Bibles, magazines,
and hymn books
piled like looted
bee boxes around
his reading chair.

There is always
some big old bear
ready to live on
even in territory broken
and abused, crossing
roads to love or feast,
berry pie either way,
hurtling forward on
mountain heart
and wild blood.
Run on. Survive.
Live long in the thickets.

About the Author

John Lane is the author of over a dozen books of poetry and prose. His *Abandoned Quarry: New & Selected Poems* was released by Mercer University Press in Macon, GA. in 2012. The book includes much of Lane's published poetry over the past 30 years, plus a selection of new poems. *Abandoned Quarry* won the SIBA (Southeastern Independent Booksellers Alliance) Poetry Book of the Year prize. Several of his latest prose books are *My Paddle to the Sea*, published by The University of Georgia Press, and *Begin With Rock, End With Water* from Mercer University Press. He teaches environmental studies at Wofford College and lives in Spartanburg, SC. His website is www.kudzutelegraph.com

Colophon

This limited edition printing of 300 copies

was set in Cambria, Papyrus and Times New Roman type

and printed on recycled and natural papers

by Lori Perkins at TPS in Newton, Illinois

in the fall of 2014.

Fifty copies are numbered & signed by the author